The Escape Artist

for Y

Acknowledgements
The Café Review, Cyphers, Dancing with Kitty Stobling: The Patrick Kavanagh Award Winners, International Quarterly, The Irish Times, Irish University Review, London Magazine, The North, Oxfam, Poetry Ireland Review, Poetry Review, Prairie Schooner, The Rialto, RTE, Scanning the Century: The Penguin Book of Poetry in the Twentieth Century, The Shop, Stand.

Previous publications
Oasis (Poolbeg Press 1982)
In The Bonsai Garden (Raven Arts Press 1988) (winner of the Patrick Kavanagh Award)

The Escape Artist is the winner of The Poetry Business Book & Pamphlet Competition

The Escape Artist

Padraig Rooney

Smith/Doorstop Books

Published 2006 by
Smith/Doorstop Books
The Poetry Business
The Studio
Byram Arcade
Westgate
Huddersfield HD1 1ND

Copyright © Padraig Rooney 2006
All Rights Reserved

ISBN 1-902382-85-4

Padraig Rooney hereby asserts his moral right to be identified as the author of this book.

British Library Cataloguing-in-Publication Data. A catalogue record for this book is available from the British Library.

Designed and typeset at The Poetry Business
Printed and bound by CPI Antony Rowe, Eastbourne
Cover picture by John Singer Sargent

Distributed by Central Books Ltd., 99 Wallis Road, London E9 5LN

The Poetry Business gratefully acknowledges the help of Arts Council England and Kirklees Culture and Leisure Services

CONTENTS

7	Blue
8	Cat
9	The Nuns at Poll an tSnámh
10	The Corncrake
11	The Go-between
12	Proust's Day
13	Ash
14	Wild Oats
15	The Names
17	The Duration of Burning
19	A Writer's Block
20	The Whirligig Dream
22	Freak
23	The Viaduct at Millau
24	The Released Starlings
25	The Escape Artist
26	The Beefcake Shot
27	The Coffin Trick
28	The Disappearing Act
29	The Impediment
30	A Shadow
31	Dance of the Eunuchs
32	The Sign Changer
33	The Window
34	The Tuning Fork

35	The Angels' Part
36	The Haircut
38	Pool
40	The White Omelette
41	Among the Sham
42	The Biretta
44	A Deeper Blue
45	The River at Mohács
46	Sonar
47	At the Pointe Courte
48	The Lay-by
49	The Sea of Nothingness
50	The Irish Rainforest
51	Tristia
52	Spa
54	The Sorrowful Mysteries

BLUE

You're eating blue marlin on a blue bayou
under a gibbous moon, years ago.
The whole journey and a Honda 50
tick over in the shade, cooling.
After dinner, after all we've been through,
come over here and tidy my eyebrows,
heap the bones on the side of the blue plate
and sing to me like you used to do
in our salad days: *Blue Angel, sotto voce.*

CAT

I was sent down to the canal –
the Royal Ulster – to drown a cat.
I'd tricked her, big with kittens,
into the sack and bunched it tight.
She fought under her dark hood,
leaping from my wrist, tigerish.
Tying the neck with twine,
reef knot and scout's clove hitch,
her fur tickled through the gunny
and her claws drew blood.
There were two steps to the water
mantled deep before the locks
where the slow barges waited
for its volume to fall.
I held her under a long time
until I'd judged her gone, but she
broke surface and my knots, roaring,
and was away over the fields
to the woods, not looking back.
I was glad she'd high-tailed
and left me with my half-guilt:
I'd tried and failed my first kill,
the sack empty and the knot undone.
The scum reformed over that look
she gave surfacing, fat with life,
as she escaped me for the trees.

THE NUNS AT POLL AN tSNÁMH

After thirty years holding their breath
they break the surface this morning,
Sisters Attracta, Concepta, Assumpta.
They're wearing flour bags gathered
by elastic at the top, unstitched below,
to shield themselves from prying eyes.
Three young nuns at *Poll an tSnámh*
undressing, fluent Irish on the wind,
the summer men landed on the moon.
Their habits, veils, coifs come off
until they're in their pelts under the bags
with *Odlums Flour* stencilled on them.
It's the only nuns' striptease we've seen,
or will ever see. They approach the edge
whiteskinned in their dark bathing suits.
They're going in, going under, disappearing
into the green water of the deep end.

THE CORNCRAKE

My father braced against the upright scythe
sharpening the blade with the sharpening stone
whetted with his sweat, and whistling the blues
like a guitarist of air on his air guitar,
like the grim reaper and Orpheus on his lyre
fused in one admonitory muse
that goes *whisht!* and cocks his head to listen
to what appears to be the far-off corncrake's
two-note adieu across the stubbled field:
and there it goes again: *crek, crek,*
going singing, gone from the natural world.

THE GO-BETWEEN

In Chartier, years ago, coming out, I engaged
the lone diner opposite in polite conversation
between mouthfuls of *chèvre*. Our stories led
to the one about André Gide happening upon
Wilde's and Bosie's names on the hotel slate
in Blidah, Algeria, in 1895. Gide erased his own
and left for the station. But, my diner pointed out,
changed his mind and returned. The seed was sown!
He laid aside his *osso bucco* to tell me Gide's
view of Wilde's use of Bosie: depraved right down
to the marrow. I had a *mystère* and my opposite
a *crême brulée*. Later, Wilde showed Gide the town
and played go-between for the little flute player:
You forgot the time and the place and who you were.

PROUST'S DAY

Some days I don't wake until night.
I summon the servants with a bell:
shaving water, stale newspapers,
café au lait piping hot, lots of it,
and croissant crumbs on the quilt.
By midnight my day takes shape
from a little light reverie, a puzzle,
the thousand pieces of a masterpiece.
I hear the church bells ring the hours,
the aerial bombardments, the all-clear.
The servants tiptoe as Mama told them
long ago, leaving trays at my door.
I might summon a sealed carriage
and ride around the dark boulevards,
pick up the scum of the aerodromes.
The squares are empty at that hour,
the men mute. I get them to talk dirty
over my pack of snaps, a royal flush
of Duchesses and Contessas, Mama
among them. I pay the butcher boys
to bring me fat rats from the abattoir,
to stick them with hatpins, beat them
round my cork-lined walls as I watch.
Once they killed a chicken as I came.
I order in *purée* and champagne,
a chamber orchestra to play Fauré,
note their eyes, their lips, the curl
of their jumped-up moustaches.
I'm in bed by nine, correcting proofs
by electric light, the shutters closed.

ASH

This first American edition of Ted Hughes's *Crow*
I found in a Forces Clearance Sale in Bangkok,

stamped all over with its ports of call: Camp Samae San,
The International Social and Recreation Club Library,

Property of the United States Army. It's due in long ago
– November 1st. 1974, the tail end of the war,

and the borrowers' names in lazy high-school print
are few and far between in that far-off decade.

But one of them left ash – a late-night joint, a savoured Camel? –
between pages 14 and 15, at 'Crow's Account of the Battle'.

Was it after those dawn missions overflying Cambodia
or pensive-sick in intensive care, recuperating,

or flaked out by the pool like me, turning the page,
when 'what was left look round at what was left?'

WILD OATS

It's twelve years after the end of the Vietnam War
on the shorefront of this old rest and recreation town,
in a singles bar full of tourists watching the whores.
It's a Sunday at the tail end of the rainy season
at the edge of the ocean with a squall coming in.

This is the life, you're thinking, the promised Shangri La,
the smut of the free world's press coming off on your hands.
Out in the bay the grey battleships are almost a mirage
and due south Quonset huts line the runways
where men of the sixties rolled joints and let loose thunder.

Across on the shingle their Amerasian sons breakdance
at the tide's edge – glue-sniffers in their early teens –
part American, part African, part Asian, conjuring rain.
They're the town's young bloods, the wild oats of war,
high on solvent years after the end of hostilities.

Who'd think it? – least of all those cheap charlies
of the grainbelt who rode out the storm in a seaside town
as countless armies before them. When they write the histories
this small mixed-race diaspora breakdancing on the shore
will be swimming out into the gene pool and almost gone –

a human-interest footnote in someone's post-war book.
Abandoned in this airbase town at the runway's end,
they're like us: disjointed, almost grown-up reminders
that the barbarians were here and have not quite gone.
We watch them dance where their fathers have flown.

THE NAMES

'The first duty of a ruler is to rectify names,'
says one of the analects of Confucius. 'If names

be not correct, language is not in accordance
with the truth of things.' I'm pedalling furiously,

saying it over and over to myself like a mantra,
up on the River Kwai in Kanchanaburi province,

downstream from the infamous bridge. Not the one
blown up by Alec Guinness in the film of that name

– a reconstructed model in Ceylon (now Sri Lanka) –
but the one pieced back together after the war.

The track runs to Three Pagodas Pass on the border
with Burma (now Myanmar), and I'm stalled at a crossing

as the rolling stock goes by, branded with R S R
– Royal Siamese Railways (present day Thailand).

It must be my first time on a bike in fifteen years,
I think, as I turn in off the road to a monastery

to rest under a tamarind tree out of the heat.
There's a clear view of the river from where I sit,

but if I turn and look back across the compound,
beyond the shunting yards, I see them ranged in rows:

the neat precisely chiselled graves of the war dead
– a score for every sleeper laid across the jungle.

And all that afternoon they're on the tip of my tongue,
like kids I've taught these fifteen years coming into view,

one by one, just as they were then, under twenty,
lined up for inspection and answering to their names.

THE DURATION OF BURNING

i

In the geisha houses of old Japan
they're snuffing out the scented time-pieces.
The duration of burning determines the price.

A Japanese man, at the moment of pleasure,
will cry out: *iku!...iku!* – I'm going,
I'm going! – touch and go –

the moment of poetry a slip of the tongue.
Of the women we know nothing: they are kept
tight-lipped and silent, watching the clock.

In China, on the other hand, in 1668,
the Jesuit Father Gabriel de Magalhaens,
clockmaker to his imperial majesty,

wrote of incense clocks 'for the literate
and travellers, all those who wish to arise
at a precise hour for some affair.'

A small weight suspended on the joss
invariably falls, when the fire arrives,
into the basin of brass below it.

Thus waking the sleeper.

ii

You're gone barely three hours. Just now
I woke from a dream in which I was travelling
thousands of miles across the dateline.

I woke with the smell of burning,
the sweet smell of devotion:
patchouli and rue, terebinth and clove.

It might have been Xanadu 'where blossomed
many an incense-bearing tree.'
Or the crest of a dune with the Magi riding it

before the slaughter of the innocents.
But I knew I had woken at a precise hour
for some affair: hours from now.

A WRITER'S BLOCK

Once I lived with a deaf-mute funambulist.
His ancestors were Chinese trapeze artists,

and a much-thumbed picture in his wallet showed
one on top of the other in an unsteady pyramid –

his extended family, and he the fall-guy summit
in spangled body-stocking, frozen in pirouette,

upside-down and not hearing a thing. So much
for a sense of balance and the hard of hearing.

He taught me the sign language for love, child,
write, read, remember – all the essentials.

He'd breakdance to the beat coming through the floor,
tensing some muscles, loosening others.

He'd flip over on the spot and do handstands,
naked, round that flat I had in Chinatown.

When we split up, his bare footprints surfaced
in the oddest places. I took to staring into space

and didn't know what to do with my hands.
There was a pregnant quality to the silence.

I balanced the brush handle on my index finger,
slept like a fakir, gripping the bolster.

An old dream returned of catching or being caught,
of stepping into thin air and landing on my feet.

THE WHIRLIGIG DREAM

i

On my first night back in the mango republic
you showed me the anatomy theatre in the dark.

Then we went back to your place and made love
under a poster of a skeleton from Hoffmann-La Roche,

all two hundred and six bones laid out and tagged
in Latin and English. Post-coital and jet-lagged,

I retold my story of wild parties with the sons
of those Basle drug barons, when I was sixteen.

After military service they drank champagne
from the barrels of their Swiss army guns.

Now I slept in arms smelling of formalin
and woke to bones littering the counterpane,

fibula, tibia, assorted ribs, a hand
reticulated like Meccano, your take-home hoard

from gross anatomy. We played knucklebones
over breakfast with some poor Yorick's knuckles

and made love again like the old times, quick,
before hitting the streets of the mango republic.

ii

Ten years of my life in this capital of sleaze,
boomtown of the East, one of the emerging democracies.

When you were small I had a recurring dream
I called the whirligig dream (my child's name

for helicopter). Returning on a rescue mission,
I hung from a rope ladder like Action Man

while you were below within arm's reach
as we lifted and whirled, making that final pitch

for freedom across the roof-top heliport.
Whether you made it or didn't make it

into the wind machine's decisive take,
I woke up sweating in the tropical dark

and called you before you went to school.
When the army opened fire outside the Royal Hotel

on the demonstrators for democracy,
among the fifty-three dead was a boy

your age, blown away under a flame tree,
while I sat at home and watched it on BBC.

FREAK

Three glider pilots gliding in the Sixties
caught the updraft and were lifted high
above the thermals into the rarefied air
where a thunderstorm tossed them further
in the thin balsaboard that held them up
so that all three baled out with their chutes
drawing them up into the storm's eye,
a freak one, where Thor's thunderclouds
sucked them into a forge of ice smiting
hailstones as big as basketballs at Earth
and wrapped those pilots in cold shrouds
that fell into our atmosphere from chutes
on brittle strings – three giant hailstones
in one of which a pilot still breathed.

THE VIADUCT AT MILLAU

That joins the Languedoc and *Langue d'Oil*
calls to mind the biblical conundrum:
was it camel (Greek *kamelos*) or cable
(*kamilos*), God's mistake or scribal pun

one afternoon in the scriptorium
when spirit wrote the world as parable,
slipped so easy through the needle's eye
and found itself inside the gates of heaven?

THE RELEASED STARLINGS

Outside the marble gates of the temple
the karma seller stands. His cages
surround him, one-bird wicker cages
the visitors to the temple pay to open
and release the starling chirping inside.
In this way the pilgrims make merit.
They make such a racket, the caged
and released starlings in the trees
along the canals by the royal palace.
And why wouldn't they break into song,
these conductors of karma, birds
whose souls fly free for a few baht?
But when the pilgrims have gone home,
the seller stands under the trees singing.
Come here little starlings, he sings,
or merely chirps, trilling his tongue.
And they fly down to him one by one
back into their cages he's left open.

THE ESCAPE ARTIST

He remembers Harry Houdini going down
into the East River and not coming up.
It was iced over the winter he changed
to long pants, so cold he'd lose his skin
touching it for a dare, for a dime.
Trussed, chained, greased and cuffed
he was bundled into a steamer trunk
and the bolts slammed home, padlocked.
'No tricks!' he's assured by bared wrists
showing the keys to his favourite stowaway.
He almost hears the tumblers click.
The whole conundrum suspended upside down
from a crane and winched into place
over a manhole in the ice a jigsaw cut.
He hauls it up and holds it there turning.
Was it watertight? Is he loose already
and only waiting for the plunge to mask
his getaway's art? He'll pick the locks
and rise to a coin of light and applause
where we wait, like him, with held breath.
Any minute now he'll bob on the surface,
back from the brink as always and game
for more. Come up, Harry! the boy shouts
in his breaking voice into the East River.
Come back to us you wily escape artist,
come back here and show us your tricks.

THE BEEFCAKE SHOT

Could I interest you, sir, in one of the early beefcake shots
taken circa 1890 when Houdini was sixteen?

Note the photographer's bossed stamp and the studio address
at 49th and Lexington. A bit soiled but in good nick.

On the back, if I may, the contortionist's bold autograph.
Note too his bandy-legged double-joints and pugilist stance.

This is one of six snaps where we see Houdini buck-naked
bar the chains. The rest remain in private hands, mostly abroad.

What's unique about this curio, sir, are the shadows of chains
across the canvas backdrop, and of the young punter himself

staring out at us handcuffed and unashamed from his own time.
In the less valuable prints the shadows are airbrushed away.

THE COFFIN TRICK

A tedious preamble during which Houdini shoots his cuffs.
The Greatest Manacle Manipulator etc. etc.

He flexes his muscles and sends a ripple through the crowd.
Straitjacket. A man from the audience double-checks the locks

while Houdini's prehensile toes extract the pick and place it
in the palm of his hand. Regulation English cuffs, locked left,

and Nova Scotia leg irons, scarce, he remarks laconically.
Opening night at the Alhambra at the century's turn.

He enters the coffin with Promethean aplomb before
getting down to work the nuts and bolts of stealthy art.

It only takes a minute. He plays patience behind the screen
for half an hour, milking it, then strolls back in to loud applause.

THE DISAPPEARING ACT

A wanted ad in *Conjurers Magazine* in 1906:
boy assistant for carney hall artiste. Brooklyn area.

Regular conjuring work was scarce then, before the Great War.
Auditions took place upstairs in a dime hall cum stripper club

called *Now You See It, Now You Don't*. His stage name was de Kolta
and all down the coast we pulled the punters with a ouija board,

did card tricks, escapes, disappearing acts: one called Pandora
a classic of its kind that sent the audience psychotic.

Boxes locked inside coffins inside trunks, while de Kolta
released the trap door, waved his wand and made me disappear.

A tense silence. I held my last breath. He clicked finger and thumb.
Ninety years ago, mister, since he said abracadabra.

THE IMPEDIMENT

After he saw dead grass snakes on the road
an extra penis grew overnight from his mouth,
the length and thickness of a boy's thumb.
It curled back on itself tactfully when he spoke,
but even so, his speech grew glottal, difficult.
The new penis had a toehold on his gum,
and a wisdom tooth hung from the raw pulp
at the end. He looked at it that first time
he shaved, and gave the dental floss a miss.
He went in to announce this new growth
to his parents. A summer of orthodontics
and therapy later, he smiled at the world.
At odd moments, though, he'd stammer
and recall how long ago he tucked back in
that extra penis, and how it complained.
Then his speech would come right again.

A SHADOW

The last eunuch, Sun Yaoting,
had served his emperor well.
Indentured at eight, castrated,
he entered the Forbidden City
of the Manchu dynasty, the court
of Pu Yi, the puppet emperor.
He guarded the concubines,
a shadow among women.
At the time of the warlords
Sun Yaoting hid in the temples.
During the Cultural Revolution
his amputated genitals were burned
in fear of the Red Guards.
His one desire was to be reunited
with his parts at the time of death,
to be reincarnated a whole man.
'When I die I will come back
as a cat or dog,' he lamented.
He died at the age of ninety-three,
the last eunuch of imperial China.

DANCE OF THE EUNUCHS

I will give them an everlasting name that shall not be cut off
Isaiah 56:36-5

The last time we clapped eyes on them they were mere boys
offered up to the puppet emperor in a long-ago winter,
boys huddled barefoot and pony-tailed by the ball alleys
quarried stone by stone from the Gobi wilderness.

Who are these old men in tasselled caps and pongee slippers
wanting to come in from the cold of the dragon economy?
We'll kowtow no longer to their backstairs intrigue, their womanly ways.
Look at them mince and lift their useless ceremonial dress.

Look how the guards bussed in from the country manhandle them
as they totter in yellow socks like fat dowagers
stitched up in stays of bone and silk. Is there no shame?
Once they were our solution, our conduit to power.

Once we might have given them our boys as their own
to raise among the mandarins of the forbidden city.
Now they stamp their slippered feet in mutinous unison
and carry their precious in jars before them for all to see.

They let their long grey hair down around their shoulders
and dance the shimmy, the swagger, the eunuch swish.
They open up their yellow parasols on Tiananmen Square
and make whoopee under the gate of divine might.

THE SIGN CHANGER

I caught him late one night
on the rue de Leningrad
up a ladder with his screws
and enamelled replacement.
He quietly put back the sign.
There's less hassle at night,
he said, I can get more done.
What do you do, I asked him,
with the remaindered ones?
– thinking I could scrounge.
O those, he said, smiling,
pointing to a knapsack-full,
go straight to the archives
on the rue des Archives,
in case they're needed.
It's swings and roundabouts
these days, he said, screwing
the rue de Peterburg home.

THE WINDOW
for Aidan

And if he looked down the long escalier
that joins rue Berthe to the rue des Trois Frères
he'd see himself vanish round the corner
in a cloud of Gauloises smoke, *sans filtre*,
like a genie shaped from the Paris air,

and by the time he climbed down the four floors
of pock-marked lino and waxed banister,
negotiated the dog-turded gutter,
the backpackers, exiles, tramps and whores,
he might second-guess: was it himself there

or only the dope-induced smoke and mirrors
of his teenage years? – were it not for
the urge to glance back up the flight of stairs
at the window he looked out of that year.

THE TUNING FORK

I'm listening to Sister Liam forty years ago
strike the tines of a tuning fork and hold it

quivering for me to hear above the piano,
ciúnas a leanbh, and to a crystal vase

on the May altar reverberating the note
and holding a bouquet of white roses

I'd cut for her that morning from the garden.
Those lovely wilting blameless tuned in-roses.

THE ANGELS' PART

The spirit lost
is called the angels' part,

la part des anges,
breaching the staves

to claim the air
and be claimed by it

at two per cent a year.
But the vintage years

they hoop and hoop again
to keep the spirit in

for leaner times
and rarer blends.

We're volatile between
these two extremes:

to let it fly away
to make it stay.

THE HAIRCUT

A week before he died
he had his hair cut.
He cracked a joke
entering the barber's
for a short back-and-sides.
'You thought I was a goner.'
A man with the same name
had died that weekend.
The barber laughed, unfolding
his white sheet, as he laughs
and unfolds it now.
All three steady customers.
They spoke then of the other
as hair fell grey and lacklustre.
My father caught himself looking
younger in that mirror there.
His namesake dogged him
all his life, and dogged him now.
He hovered between my father,
the barber and the mirror,
like the glances there, sizing up.
He'd a good innings, they concluded.
And for a minute, I like to think,
my father let his head rest
on this leather headrest, thinking,
looking at the blue and green bottles,
those dangling strops and razors,
seeing his own end not far off.
And that was his last haircut.
A week to the day, the barber
tells me, my father, too, was gone.
I lean back on the headrest
with my eyes closed, then open,

looking in the mirror
at the mirror in the barber's hand.

POOL

> *There's always a pool parlor wherever one goes
> (think I'll use this line in a poem) if one gets bored.*
> Elizabeth Bishop, *One Art: Letters*

There's always a pool parlour wherever one goes.
I travel light, with a two-bit screw-together cue
in this customised case, my monogram worked
into the Italian leather. I looked like a hitman,
or woman, in the old days, stepping off the trains
into a scuzzy underworld where I'd play pool,

professionally, for money – in those station pool
parlours cum barbershops where the Mafia goes.
I'd chat up hoods in the smokers of the trains –
faggot amateur, they'd think, fingering my screwy cue,
but time and again they fell for it to a man.
My smooth-faced con-trick always worked.

In these Med towns the men are over-worked
or on the dole. Either way they're game for pool.
I loved the crack of the break, the man-to-man
lickety-split of the shoeshine boy as he goes
about his blow-job in the john, the tick of the cue
in smoke-blue parlours underneath the trains.

Ah, those runaway cross-dressers riding the trains
with stiletto hearts and false eyelashes. They'd worked
nights since they were boys and could come right on cue!
On bank holiday weekends we'd celebrate and pool
our stakes, live it up in Naples or in Rome. Money goes
quickly with low-life Romeos. I took it like a woman,

but where it mattered I potted them like a man,
one by one under the arriving and departing trains,

the reds, the yellows, the blues. Luck comes and goes
but with me it's skill in adversity that's always worked,
the hormone rush that comes with beating men at pool
I've had since I was twelve, and chalked my first cue.

My Scrabble dictionary says it's a variation of *queue*.
You wouldn't care to play to pass the time, young man?
I'm a dab hand at Scrabble, but nothing like I am at pool,
and we've hours to kill before we board our trains.
Truth is, my con-man tricks haven't really worked
in these *termini* for years. Youth too comes and goes,

like a cue-ball potting back and forth in sixteen goes.
I'm worked to death these days picking up a man,
and a spot of pool might do the trick until our trains.

THE WHITE OMELETTE

In the scullery the pan without a handle
gripped by an oven glove on one hand

the white omelette lamenting its yolk
but sliding nonetheless effortlessly

onto the heirloom willow pattern plate
where the young lovers in their houseboat

(Koong-shee the beautiful daughter and Chang
the impoverished scholar) are becoming

bluebirds arguably singing out of harm's way
across that crack there in the old china.

AMONG THE SHAM

The shamans took the frightened boys aside
in forest clearings ringed by wattle huts
that backed on playing fields, as though a god

might land, a trinity, a pantheon
whose graven images were set in alcoves
in dung-coloured walls. The boys went down

on bended knee and made burnt offerings
in clouds of incense, learned by heart the rules
of dead and dying tribal languages,

prayed on dried seeds of hollowed gourds
wearing talisman and scapular,
and faced the wooden altars where shrunken heads

looked out at them from gilded reliquaries,
elders of the tribe or former shamans.
And so the young they hid among the trees

were shamans in their turn who watched the boys
for signs of god. A puerile beauty helped,
and prowess on the playing field, or a voice

crying in the wilderness or coming
from the trees that said its name was Sham.
The people of the tribe gave up their young

in forest clearings ringed by wattle huts
where shamans claimed they heard the voice of god
and firmly took the frightened boys aside.

THE BIRETTA

An old priest does time
in the cells of my mind

in the cells of the body
looks out a high window

coaxes birds, teases memory
all day I've looked him in the face

wee priest, singing priest
old parish shaman

dying out in our karaoke
and condom culture

with the nuns in a Mini
and his talk-show fame

goes back to Fifties Ireland
in a Marian year

rockeries and rookeries
all that dark lovely clart

fingering the silks
of a rain-buckled breviary

old foxy foxed by time
walks out under whitethorn

after benediction in drumlin country
opening for him, releasing him

like a plain five-bar gate
in slo-mo he lifts

his biretta in one hand
(missal tucked under

his oxter) and throws it
high in the prelapsarian air

the gift of prayer
he thinks: the biretta

coming back down into
our cupped uplifted hands.

A DEEPER BLUE

The intense blue of the kingfisher
on his branch on the Via Domitia
before diving into the river's blue.

I was a centurion on the bridge
between one posting and another
in the province of the Narbonensis.

It shook with the chariots crossing,
but held, our Roman engineering
rippling the river. I thought of you –

the deep blue border of your toga
put by, my boy, for the toga virilis,
and leaned over the bridge to catch

the kingfisher's rise, a deeper blue
rippling the blue ripples of the river.

THE RIVER AT MOHÁCS

for Joanna France Lewis

The Danube is so still you wouldn't think
the current strong enough to pull the ferry
across. But here it comes, *The Esmerelda*,

letting down its prow to show a truck
and three pre-capitalist cars – Trabants,
almost retro, patched with polyfilla.

The boatman sports an anchor on his cap
and counts his change. A Hell's Angel pulls
a grey ponytail outside his leather jacket

and mounts a vintage Harley whose sidecar
contains four cockerels in a wicker cage.
He guns the engine and they disembark.

Nothing moves for an hour on the slipway.
A woman at a window shakes a teacloth.
A man attempts to sell us purple plums.

Across the river boys are skinny-dipping.
Mohács sleeps in the heat. *The Esmerelda*
putters out to where the catfish are biting.

SONAR

after Thomas Moore

Believe me if I tell you the bats are blind
        and guided by instinct and sonar
out of their cave mouth into the warm night wind
        in search of fruit; that they're older
than the temple honouring their coming and going
        where monks for thousands of years
have sung mantras and sutras under the wings
        of millions winnowing the air;

and if I tell you all this exotica will pass
        and your endearing young charms
slacken to the texture of bat wings, your face
        wizen, your voice squeak, your sight grow dim;
that dinosaurs come down to us as scavenging birds
        on this darkening plain; that love
is our only sonar and song – would it not beggar
        belief or would you believe?

AT THE POINTE COURTE
in memory of Mary Reid

The road turns off the dual carriageway
to a carpark under a suspension bridge
that lifts to let the boats into the marina.

Claim a bollard and watch the shadow play
of weeds on hull, of salty men at the bar
clicking dominoes or worry beads.

Saunter down the quays named after jousters
and socialists, kept tidy by fishwives
tending geraniums in old tin cans.

The cats will stare as though they see a ghost
but nothing here has changed: the same lagoon
with stakes and ghats suspending pots of squid

in salt water above Phoenician mud;
the same indifferent waves that saw the Greeks
and then the Romans routed; the ebb tide

gathering momentum, falling short of land;
the tramontane that ushers in the cold
and fog along the Languedoc tonight.

THE LAY-BY

At the side of this road in upstate New York
a boy sells Coon cheese, a rare American cheddar,

under a hand-painted sign that drips in the heat.
I pull in and he serves me a wedge on a paper plate,

washed down by home-made cider from the freezer.
Its wire trails off into scrub and the national grid.

He pares the rind with a clasp knife in his paint-stained fingers
and tells me he's full-blooded Pawnee. I believe him.

He crouches under a cedar tree that lends its oil to the cheese
and watches me eat. He has one brown eye and one green.

We might have painted this lay-by with our own hands:
the tar-paper shack at the end of the trail to the orchard,

the paintbrush standing at an angle in a jar of turps.

THE SEA OF NOTHINGNESS

> *Free in the oriental streets of thought*
> Patrick Kavanagh

The North Road is like an eastern bazaar
through which we walk arm in arm
among pans and woks and coriander
in the stink of durian on the warm air.

It is the rainy season in Monaghan
and we are anxious to get home
before the Shambles is under water
and the town gridlocked with sampans.

We meet my mother in the temple
clutching a ticket and watching a wheel
that goes round and round like karma,
while my father rakes the marble gravel

in perfect circles round our cherry tree
under stars named for gods and emperors.

THE IRISH RAINFOREST

Algae turn the tide to blood and sand
rains from heaven out of the Sahara.
Demented with heat and bites, the men
sing sea shanties and itch at the crotch.
Bosun rations rum to a dram a day.
The tangled creeper smells of vase water
and nests large birds resembling our crake.
At sunrise we tack below the cliffs that end
in mangrove unearthed above the tide –
awash with wrack, snake-infested, the mud
giving off gas and plopping with leeches.
The enormous green not without beauty.
The men report shoals of whiskered fish
the length of a man, beating tails against
the battened hatches, drumming to be let in.
The air so fertile pollen dusts the clothes
and fungus turns the bindings back to skin.
Bosun spies a tower's broken teeth
and a pack of tigers camouflaged in green
turning to face us on the blood-red tide.
These are the great Irish tigers mentioned
in the chronicles, hitherto thought extinct.

TRISTIA

This line runs to the Black Sea and surfaces
at a suite of stations named after Ovid's *Tristia*,
the platforms right at the water's edge on pylons
sunk in mangrove swamp, the swollen tide
a primal soup of brine, near daybreak, moonstruck,
tannoys crackling to life at the train's approach
and announcing the names in impeccable Latin,
an index of first lines, last poems, *termini*,
disembodied, dying in the dead language,
no-one getting on or off, the wheels clattering
in the tunnels between stops, the marshland
quiet except for the squawking of big birds
that skim the black surface with a wingtip
and nest who knows where once night falls.

SPA

In this southern town along the isthmus
hot springs bubble under the jungle,
forming pools of sulphurous water. Eggs boil
beside their boilers neck-deep in heat,
deep heat, and red children run from pool
to pool, testing the spa temperatures:
tepid, hot, hotter, scalding at the source.

Casinos keep the nouveau riche on edge
and beauty parlours pamper the women:
heat treatment, mud and hydrotherapy.
And down the overgrown border lanes
little ramshackle brothels hold out
against encroaching jungle, the foreign
indentured whores lightly boiled, soiled,

past their sell-by date. Along the quays,
rats investigate discarded fish
and cats look out to sea at winking lights
where smugglers to and fro in darkened junks
between disputed islands, named on maps
for sea captains, opium merchants,
loggers and queens; named differently

by those who toil in the small coastal town,
or boil rather, like the succulent blue crabs
which are its special dish. The spa hotels
are full of tattooed, pot-bellied cops
swapping crimes in the pool, and minor wives
of local big-wigs sunk in plopping mud,
their cucumber eyes facing the sun.

You might think the whole town's about to blow.
Lizards tiptoe from stone to burnished stone.
The scorched volcanic hills give off smoke.
In the market, vats of boiling fat cook
stick insects and greasy knobs of dough.
Each year the sea rises a centimetre,
the mean temperature gets hotter.

THE SORROWFUL MYSTERIES

In a lay-by smelling of tar and nettles
a rain barrel simmered on low heat,
abandoned by the county council
or a caravan of gypsies just decamped

leaving flattened grass and glowing embers.
Whores in hot pants and fishnet stockings,
on stacked heels of leatherette and cork,
stood under the lights of the hard shoulder

as articulated trucks braked and pulled in.
Ethnic cleansing had given way to peace
and grants, the millennium had come and gone,
and my beetle morphed to a limousine

down the long middle-European roads
of houses and custard-coloured outhouses,
where the old collective farms stretched
to a horizon of flood plain and black earth,

where boys pedalled out to look at cattle
and men to look at stills along the river.
I sensed them behind me on the back seat
and crowding out the rear-view mirror –

Teasie's pillbox hat with netting trim,
my smuggler uncle's handlebar moustache
clotted with snuff, hair slick with Brylcreem,
Imelda in her Aran wool poncho,

my mother under a Lourdes mantilla
and my father passing round Sweet Afton
in the dark recesses of the hackney car.
Patsy Cline (or was it Dolly Parton?)

came over the airwaves from Hilversum,
then decade after decade of the rosary,
the sorrowful mysteries in perfect rhythm,
each one vivid as a line of poetry.

My father said the last decade in Irish,
tagged on a plethora of trimmings
and the evening raga of Catholic prayer
filled the limousine with grief and droning.

'All the popes in my time were good popes,'
intoned Teasie the moment they were done
stowing beads into bags and glove box.
Polo mints were passed from hand to tongue

and my granny conjured up the Montenegrin
Reids coming down out of their mountain
fastness into the Drina plain, the pied-noir
Rooneys from Galicia and the Ukraine,

rabbis, sons of rabbis, pogrom survivors
made good in the dark shtetls of empire.
Stories crossed and interwove like mourners
at a funeral, breaking into lament,

then into Kaddish, Yiddish, banshee wails,
the whole gamut of keening filling the car
running on empty through the Balkan night.
From the back came a pedal steel guitar,

Ruby, Tammy, Maybelle and Darlene Reid,
gypsy queens with klezmer horns and sax
played fusion beats where Patsy Cline left off.
The border road led to a jerrybuilt bridge

and a greasy spoon neither here nor there
in no-man's land, contested, fluorescent lit,
peopled by night-hawks and hitchhikers
eyeing each other up for a bed or a lift.

Here they all got out and stretched their legs.
A low-hulled ferry plied the swollen river,
a smell of diesel and hard-boiled eggs
unwrapped, cracked, peeled and dipped in salt.

A kettle set to boil on a petrol primus,
a Tetrapac of milk and Tupperware
filled with cooked ham and lamb and lettuce
sandwiches appeared out of nowhere,

the plaid rug laid for a picnic in the dark
levitated like my hijackers
hurrying now to cross the ferry car park
that sloped towards the oil-slicked water.